CW01312875

First published in 2022 by Will and Co, Bard in the Yard and Amazon Kindle Publishing.

Will Shakes and Co
Westbourne Mansions, 148-150 Sandgate Road, CT20 2HS Folkestone
www.willandco.co.uk

Bard in the Yard
The Flat, St Mary's Parish Centre, St. Marys Road, Bodmin, England, PL31 1NF
www.bardintheyard.co.uk

Copyright @ Victoria Gartner, 2022

UKCCS Copyright for King Leonardo, His Three Daughters and Their Dog by Victoria Gartner: number 284737054, since 2020.

UKCCS Copyright for The Scottish Play: number 284740935, since 2021.

Victoria Gartner is hereby identified as author of these plays in accordance with section 77 of the Copyright, Designs and Patents Act 1988. The author has asserted her moral rights.

All rights whatsoever in these plays are strictly reserved and application for performance etc. should be made before commencement of rehearsal to Bard in the Yard Ltd, The Flat, St Mary's Parish Centre, St. Marys Road, Bodmin, England, PL31 1NF (charlie@willandco.co.uk). No performance may be given unless a license has been obtained, and no alterations may be made in the title or the text of the play without the author's prior written consent.

You may not copy, store, distribute, transmit, reproduce or otherwise make available this publication or any part of it in any form, or binding or by any means (print, electronic, digital, optical, mechanical, photocopying, recording or otherwise), without the prior written permission of the publisher. Any person who does any unauthorized act in relation to this publication may be liable to criminal prosecution and civil claims for damages.

ISBN: 9798828122578

Cover by Victoria Gartner, Design by Christopher Commander

Visit bardintheyard.co.uk for more information.

Bard in the Yard

King Leonardo
&
The Scottish Play

VICTORIA GARTNER

DEDICATION

This is to everyone who has ever had a crazy dream,
and to the friends who have helped them make that dream a reality.

CONTENTS

Acknowledgments	i
Introduction	1
Prologue	7
King Leonardo	12
The Scottish Play	42
About the Author	87

ACKNOWLEDGMENTS

Bard in the Yard would not have been possible without many passionate, devoted, and incredibly talented artists.

We thank all the Bards. This would not have been the same without Adam Morgan, Alice Merivale, Alix Dunmore, Arron Greechan, Ben Galpin, Brigid Lohrey, Caroline Mathison, Charlie Clee, Christopher Commander, Constanza Ruff, Emma Nihill, Hannah Young, Henry Charnock, Honey Gabriel, Jonathan Blakeley, Jonathan McGarrity, Kate Roche, Kaya Bucholc, Kit McGuire, Lin Sagovsky, Lucy Aarden, Luke Farrugia, Michael Southwark, Miztli Rose, Natalie Harper, Rosanna Turner, Rupert Sadler, Sulin Hasso, and Will Harrison-Wallace.

Bard in the Yard is first and foremost an amazing team, who went above and beyond to ensure that this project would always be the best it could be. Thank you Aaron Blackledge, Beatrice Lawrence, Charlie Mackellar, Erin Rooney, Hannah Elsy, Jack Spencer, Katherine Moran, Runa Røstad Augdal, Tim Atkinson and Victoria Gartner.

Our heartfelt thanks go to our Godmother, Dame Helen Mirren.

Special thanks go to people who took a chance on us: Dominic Cavendish, Roisin O'Connor, Dr. Anjna Chouhan, Ben Crystal, Sandy Campbell, Michelle Terry, Jon Dollin and all the team at Southwark Cathedral, Sean Turner, and the team at Canal Café Theatre.

Thank you to Dutch Bard Wim Bouwens.

Thank you to Cam Harle, Christopher Commander, Sean O'Connor and Mark Woodward for capturing the magic.

Thank you to you, our audience. We did all of this for you, and we would do it again in a heartbeat. Thank you for letting us entertain you in your yard.

INTRODUCTION

By Dominic Cavendish

Bard in the Yard: not just a script, but a document for the ages of a tour de force fightback against 2020's theatrical doom and gloom.

It's almost fading into the haze of a dream, or rather, an involuntary shudder at a hair-whitening nightmare: that protracted period when the unthinkable happened and theatres were closed, a misfortune felt particularly acutely during the opening round of collective bewilderment.

Shell-shocked days after March 16 2020 turned into dumb-struck weeks; an awareness that the darkness was set to last months, if not years, grew. 'A plague on both your houses' had sat for centuries as a quaint figure of speech. At a stroke, Covid-19 brought home the reality of that curse, its mortal connotation and implied ruination. Of course the health emergency – and daily news of personal tragedies – took centre-stage, but the related suspension of a regular pastime, theatre-going - now rendered out of reach, at best an 'online' activity – was a huge shock.

The theatre 'houses' in Shakespeare's day were shut by the authorities for protracted periods, including late 1592 and throughout 1593 – not so very long before *Romeo and Juliet* was composed, circa 1595/6; plague furthermore is an integral part of the plot that prevents a messenger reaching Romeo to keep him up to speed with Juliet's feigned death.

In due course, the National staged a 'lockdown' R&J, with Josh O'Connor and Jessie Buckley, broadcast about a year into the pandemic. Way before that, though, Bard in the Yard affirmed – daringly, in the flesh – just how much Shakespeare had become 'our contemporary' (to borrow the Polish critic Jan Kott's famous phrase). The brain-child of Victoria Gartner, artistic director of the Shakespeare-oriented Will & Co, this cleverly portable, and mass-enactable, one-person show couldn't have been more creatively or socially apposite that peculiar summer.

Amid a wilderness where once there had been plenty, it was the first significant green shoot of theatrical possibility, presented within days of the Government finally giving the go-ahead for outdoor performances, with social distancing, from July 11.

As the published text makes clear, it contained a good and topical *Romeo and Juliet* gag, anachronistically rejigging a line from the play to nod to the present malady. 'Will', conceived as inspiration-bereft, and plague-constrained, interacts with an audience-member, trying to use a snatch of an old hit to get the juices flowing: "Oh that I were a glove upon that hand, / For health and safety reasons that I might touch that cheek."

And there was plenty more wit where that came from. I particularly enjoyed: "Since the bakers in Southwark have all closed, I've also made a lot of sourdough bread. I've binged the entire works of Ovid, Seneca, Cicero and Holinshed." Just prior to the pandemic, but felled by it, Ben Elton's *Upstart Crow* had come into the West End as the reigning monarch of Bardic bio-spoof. It's no hyperbole, though, to say that the comedy value was just as pronounced in Gartner's script.

And the latter felt more like a collector's item. A playful fancy that was previously an indulgence for waggish minds, Shakespeare-steeped or not, had become a play for today. The writer's block conceit – familiar also from Stoppard's *Shakespeare in Love* – achieved a rare urgency; the immortal genius's own presumed and plausible moments of creative crisis meeting with our own need to rekindle theatre, find a way forward.

One obvious difference between 2020 and 1605 – another annus horribilis for plague, closing playhouses, and resulting, so it has been much suggested, in *King Lear*, conceived here as a work-in-progress called *King Leonardo* – was that back then there was no professional commentariat. For a critic trying to earn a crust in the pandemic, gratitude doesn't come close to describing what one felt about those striving to ensure that the show must go on.

I remember hastily trying to track down Gartner on the phone, when the news of her venture was announced, much as if a new play by Pinter had been discovered. The journalistic tag-line immediately formed – thanks to a handful of other like-minded projects in the offing – of 'Deliveroo theatre'. From that flowed some immediately interesting thoughts on how theatre as a form might reconnect, at a grass-roots level, with its audience. Here was the most elemental form of community theatre, in theory – providing a 'to-your-doorstep' service for those stuck at home.

It felt like a fascinating throwback to the peripatetic nature of theatre in Shakespeare's day, especially during plague outbreaks in London. And the core proposition – one actor harnessing the imagination of the audience – felt like a provocative reminder about the 'O for a Muse of fire' essence of theatre.

Gartner and I talked for 20 minutes or so, during which she cheerily declared she'd had the inspiration during one of her daily walks and "like an insane person" had decided to make it happen, with the help of her producer Charlie Mackellar, in the first instance as a means of getting her industry back into work and out of its negative spiral of despair and complaint. Even with the best Will in the world, good ideas can dwindle in execution, and I was primarily glad to be out of the house, and visiting someone else's, when I headed to Stratford, East London, on July 18th to watch my first live, in-person performance since March 16th.

It's no lie to say, though, that I will remember the hour spent in the company of Jonathan Blakeley, the first of dozens of actors to deliver the script that summer, for years to come. Here, in a small patch of garden, was an affirmation of the power and courage of actors per se – horribly denigrated in some corners of Government during the darkest days of that summer; and here was the miracle cure needed for a heavy heart. It felt as if this one little show didn't just let the handful of us watching it suspend disbelief, as we had been able to do as a matter of course before; it created a higher level of appreciation and connection. A lot of talk flew around at that time about our 'human' need for storytelling; suddenly, you felt that on the bone. Equally, assumptions about individual genius ever float to the fore; here was a reminder that 'nothing will come of nothing', society feeds us.

A profound work of art? In itself, sure, it was 'only' a divertissement, but the freshness and colloquial looseness of the material was an achievement in itself given the pressures of the moment. As a marker of what was possible in impossible circumstances, it deserves being preserved as a document for the ages, as well as a source of passing entertainment in its own right. The fact that Gartner produced a follow-up, which I didn't alas see at the time, but have since read, was even more impressive. Everyone was flagging in 2021. Rather than flogging a dead horse, she was still pressing the case for coltish energy.

'Necessity is the mother of invention' is a cliché exemplified by desperate times. Theatre can have it tough in the best of years. I hope no future generation of artists has to come up with the goods, in such a frantic fashion. But there are long-term ramifications to be found in these pages about the kind of theatre we venerate, and the kind of practitioners who get supported. Ronald Harwood subtitled his biography of the actor-manager Donald Wolfit – *His Life and Work in the Unfashionable Theatre*; Wolfit, the great pedlar of Shakespeare in the provinces, and a heroic rallier for him as a national figurehead through his wartime performances, was self-financed, on the margins, and to some extent sniffily under-appreciated.

Shakespeare is lavishly supported in some parts of the subsidised sector, but we would do well to remember – and Bard in the Yard was proof positive – that the biggest beasts can be outshone by the smallest players. As a logistical feat, an artistic boon and a social and professional 'good', a venture like this warrants official acknowledgment even if it couldn't hope to get full state support. All told, it afforded memorable delight by the yard. To quote Hamlet, 'For this relief, much thanks.'

Dominic Cavendish
24 April 2022

PROLOGUE

By Victoria Gartner

It all started with Covid. It all started with fear, frustration, time on my hands and a meme. It all started on a pebble beach in Sandgate, Kent.

The world had been put on hold for two months already. My world had been turned upside down: I was out of London and living by the sea, I had moved in with my very fresh relationship, and I had got – and very slowly recuperated from – the dreaded illness. The theatre tour we were about to plan with my theatre company Will & Co was moot, as was the whole industry.

But sitting there on that beach, on that particular sunny day in May 2020, I thought: 'no.' No, I won't stand for it. No, there must be a way around this. There must be something we can do. There must be something I can do. I had moved to the UK only two years prior to that moment, after more than a decade of wanting to make work here, in Shakespeare's own homeland and its thriving and inspiring theatre scene. And I had finally done it – I had uprooted my life because of love for the Bard. And now the world was telling me there would be no more shows for the foreseeable future. No. This was simply not acceptable. You see, I had a plan, and that plan certainly did not involve *not* making theatre.

My partner had just gifted me a wonderful book that I highly recommend to any expat: *Watching the English* by Kate Fox. The chapter about front gardens in particular – and their exclusively decorative function – stuck with me.

'But of course, this country is full of front gardens!' I thought excitedly. 'As well as back gardens! There are just plenty of outdoor spaces everywhere!'

So, the usually full theatres are are now closed. But that does not mean that the audience has disappeared. They are just… at home. They are in their gardens. The back ones, of course. Let us find our audience again. Let us find the people hungry for stories, for entertainment, for connection, and let us go to them. Let us bring something our company can do well, and can do quickly: Shakespeare.

When I got back from my daily walk, I immediately phoned my friend and producer Charlie Mackellar to explain the brilliant idea I had just had: *Shakespeare in Your Park*. Thankfully, that name was later workshopped by the team and turned into *Bard in the Yard*. But for now, here it was: the germ of an idea.

It is thanks to not only Charlie's enthusiasm but also her deeply-rooted belief that 'This is important. We have to do this,' that the project truly got underway. As I was explaining it to her, I kept seeing the mountain of work it would take to accomplish something like what we had in mind, and to accomplish it remotely well.

Within two weeks of that fated afternoon, we had assembled an incredible team – here's looking at you Jack, Bee, Kayti and Tim – and sent out a casting call Tweet on 23 May 2020 mentioning people had to be based in London, be good at Shakespeare, and that this was a paid opportunity. Our small, fringe company's Twitter account exploded.

I started writing a script as we auditioned about 160 actors over Zoom. For many of them, that was their first online audition. We could not even tell them what exactly this project was, or how it would work, as we did not want the rug being pulled from under our feet and a more wealthy and experienced company to steal our idea (although we wouldn't mind selling it to you now, Andrew Lloyd Weber). We eventually revealed it all to the actors we selected: you will have to learn a solo show on Zoom and then go by yourself to a stranger's house to perform it. Thankfully, some of these artists were still in. Some had to decline because of health or caring duties. These were very strange times, indeed.

Now that twenty-two actors expected me to provide them with a script, I just about managed to finish a draft on the eve of our first read-through. From the start, it really mattered to me as a director that each Bard would be different, that each of these stellar performers would be able to put their own spin on William Shakespeare. For a solo show is a strange and wondrous thing, but it is also a terrifying ordeal. There is no one out there to help you if you lose energy, or if you lose yourself. There is only you – and the audience.

As I was writing it, we had a lot of team meetings. It was important to everyone that this project be above all a conversation. That if people were going to give us an opportunity to come to their house in the midst of a global pandemic, we would honour that trust by offering them what we had all been missing the most: connection.

After four weeks of rehearsals, we sent our very first Bard into the world: Miztli Rose performed *King Leonardo* for three theatre critics in the corner of a small London park, chaperoned by a friend of the team who made a lovely sign to announce that there was a performance in progress. At that moment in time, the rules stated that you could not meet with more than five people outdoors. And we always respected the rules.

Miztli got some lovely reviews, but the launch still felt quieter than what we had hoped for, or expected. Until one day when a shrieking Beatrice Lawrence, our press officer and associate producer, called me: 'Dominic Cavendish wants to talk to you.'

After a somewhat surreal interview in which I managed to compare our Shakespeare deliveroo project to a first date, the anticipated feature was set to come out and we all kept refreshing that page, nerve-wracked. It is not an overstatement to say it changed the course of our history. After The Telegraph called us a 'grassroots revolution,' other national newspapers followed, and bookings soared – Michelle Terry, Shakespeare's Globe own artistic director, ordered a Bard for her yard. We had truly launched.

That year, we played 57 shows.

My favourite memories are mainly of moments I did not get to be at, but that made our vertiginous amount of work worth it: the eleven-year-old's birthday party at which our Bard arrived to find all the children were dressed up in Elizabethan costumes; the tropically hot afternoon of performances in the gardens of Southwark cathedral; the older lady who had not been able to see relatives in months because she was at risk, who ordered a Bard for her birthday – she sat on her balcony while our actor performed the entire show just for her, down in her garden. The wedding anniversary. The surprise party. The barbecues, rooftop dinners, pub lunches one of our Bards got to be at. I felt each one in my heart, even though I was at home. Our actors brought smiles to people's faces and tears to their eyes. They brought them a respite, a brief moment during which we could all forget our woes for a while and suspend time, breathe in the fresh air. Each of these smiles is something I will forever be proud of.

In 2021, since the infamous meme stated that Shakespeare wrote *King Lear* and *Macbeth* in plague quarantine, and since we did not seem to be quite rid of this pestilence, I decided to write a new show: *The Scottish Play*. We also decided to take barding to a new level by going nation-wide: we had Bards in Bristol, Kent, Liverpool, Stratford-upon-Avon, Edinburgh and of course London. It was an exciting new challenge for the team. Some of our actors now had two one-hour solo shows embedded in their brains. 2021 was also the year Dame Helen Mirren kindly agreed to become our Godmother – news that I welcomed by screaming and then sobbing incoherently on the floor before rushing out to buy a bottle of bubbly.

Bard in the Yard has now been performed by 29 Bards all over the UK, by school pupils, and by the actor Wim Bouwens in Dutch in the Netherlands. *King Leonardo* and *The Scottish Play* have toured in yards, by ponds, on boats, on a jetty, online, in churches, pubs and theatres of course, but also in parking lots, care homes, offices and village halls. I do not know yet what the future holds for the Bard, but I am certain that it will be full of surprises – and hopefully, even more smiles.

Victoria Gartner
24 May 2022

KING LEONARDO

A new play by Victoria Gartner

As William Shakespeare Alice Merivale
Alix Dunmore
Ben Galpin
Charlie Clee
Constanza Ruff
Emma Nihill
Hannah Young
Henry Charnock
Honey Gabriel
Jonathan Blakeley
Jonathan McGarrity
Kate Roche
Kaya Bucholc
Kit McGuire
Lin Sagovsky
Lucy Aarden
Luke Farrugia
Michael Southwark
Miztli Rose
Natalie Harper
Rupert Sadler
Will Harrison-Wallace

Directed by Victoria Gartner

Produced by Charlie Mackellar

Associate producers Beatrice Lawrence
Jack Spencer
Katherine Moran
Tim Atkinson

West Midlands Promoter Hannah Elsy Productions

World Premiere
July 2020

Produced by Will Shakes and Co

KING LEONARDO

When arriving, please use a selection of:

Good day to you!

Lovely to meet you too, I'm Will. Is all well with you?

Could you perchance direct me to the appointed yard? Or garden?

I thank you kindly for your pains.

What a lovely place you have here! This is a most suitable and odorous orchard!

This garden shall be my stage – yes, strange times we live in. Very strange indeed. But the shows must go on.

You may now be seated. I pray you, make yourselves at home. Pour yourselves a flagon or two of wine, and some light ale for the children.

No, not for me I thank you kindly – I never partake to drink when I am on the job.

Are we all met? Are we all set?

o for a muse of fire / that would ascend[1]

the brightest heaven of invention /

a kingdom for a stage / princes to act /

and monarchs to behold the swelling scene /

then should the warlike Harry / like himself /

assume the port of Mars / and at his heels /

leashed in / like hounds should famine / sword / and fire

crouch for employment / but pardon / gentles all /

the flat unraised spirits / that have dared /

on this unworthy scaffold / to bring forth

so great an object / can this (describe the space cockpit) hold

the vasty fields of France / or may we cram

within this wooden o / the very casques

that did affright the air at Agincourt /

o pardon / since a crooked figure may

attest in little place a million /

and let us / ciphers to this great account /

on your imaginary forces work /

suppose within the girdle of these walls

are now confined two mighty monarchies /

whose high / upreared / and abutting fronts /

the perilous narrow ocean parts asunder /

piece out our imperfections with your thoughts /

into a thousand parts divide one man /

and make imaginary puissance /

think when we talk of horses / that you see them

---

[1] The Shakespeare excerpts have purposefully been left formatted as we used them in rehearsal. This method has been adopted by Victoria after a workshop with director Robert Icke. It consists of completely erasing the punctuation, which is a modern construct chosen by editors, and go back to the Folio of Shakespeare's works instead. Whenever there is a punctuation mark in the Folio, we signal it with a dash. This allows the actors to access Shakespeare's original rhythm more freely.

printing their proud hoofs i'th' receiving earth /
for 'tis your thoughts that now must deck our kings /
carry them here and there / jumping o'er times /
turning th' accomplishment of many years
into an hour-glass / for the which supply /
admit me chorus to this history /
who prologue-like / your humble patience pray /
gently to hear / kindly to judge our play /

We presume the audience applauds. If they do not, bow until they do.

Thank you, thank you. A classic—one of my greatest hits, Henry V.

A pause. Listening in.
Then, upset.

And yet… still nothing! Nothing, nothing. And nothing can come of nothing.
You see, when I am lacking inspiration, this one usually works. It triggers… well, something! It calls upon the Muse of Fire, for goodness sake!
But I forget my manners – I do entreat your graces to pardon me. Allow me to introduce myself: I am Master William Shakespeare, poet, playwright, actor, and businessman. But you can call me "The Bard" – everyone does.
What am I doing in your yard, I hear you ask?
I need to write a new play. And I am stuck.
Like, really stuck.
Like, blank parchment stuck.
Well, in these dark and dreary times of plague in our beloved London, the playhouses have been closed for many long months by the Master of the

Revels. So, we players have had to do what we could – some have fled to the countryside, some joined the King in his palace (the lucky lumpish hugger-muggers!), and some of us had to stay home in the city.

The reason I came all the way here is because you're a perfect sample of my usual audience, the smelly pick-pockety raucous rogues of Bankside, and I thought that, you know, if you're not too busy, you could help out a friend? So here I am, standing in your yard. I have introduced myself, and what might you be called, gentles?

Ask for their names.

Well, lovely to meet you, dear [name], [name] and [name]. Absolutely delightful to meet you all! If you do a good job today at helping me reignite the Bard-blockbuster-machine, I promise I shall credit you in my play's Prologue, and thus give you access to eternal fame! The unfortunate news is that if the play is a complete flop, your name might be a tad tarnished as it goes down in history.

What's that, [name]? I'm afraid you don't get a share of the profits, no. I'm forbidden by the rest of the team to hire any more associates. But the diligent clapping of fervent fans should be enough of a recompense, should it not?

So, we need to write a masterpiece, that much is clear.
So far, I've got…

Long pause.

Well, I've got a title: "King Lear" — urgh, no, sorry, that's not even a real name. Think, Will!

"King Leonardo" — Yes! Leonardo sounds most fetching. Oh, I can already see the ladies fawning all over Leonardo! — "his… Three

Daughters and…" and that's it.

Every time the plague strikes, all I hear is "Ovid wrote The Metamorphoses in quarantine, what are you doing with your time?"
By Jupiter! Thanks, that's really helpful.
These past few months, as far as productivity goes, I have: stayed in my room and slept. Made some wax candles – that's creative alright, that counts! – written some letters to my wife back home – it's incredible how people stuck in a plague are like: let's write letters every day! But that's where I do my work, you know, so sometimes at the end of a long hard day spent staring at a piece of parchment, the last thing I want to do is spend more time staring at a piece of parchment, even if it's to write to my friends! Honestly, I'm starting to get these really bad headaches from all that time spent staring at a piece of parchment. Since the bakers in Southwark have all closed, I've also made a lot of sourdough bread. I've binged the entire works of Ovid, Seneca, Cicero and Holinshed. The last season of the chronicles was not very good, but I read it anyway – that's how bad this is getting.

In the meantime, Ben Jonson's published a pamphlet in which he claims to get up every morning and eat a whole chicken, then go for a vigorous run around the Tower, write at least three scrolls of parchment to "keep it flowing, you know", practice archery in his yard, pen a few sonnets to one of his mistresses, and finally eat a whole duck while drinking a tankard of ale before going to bed. Ugh—Ben!

Alright, so – I need to up my play game, otherwise when theatres are allowed to reopen the whole company is going to be crushed in this economic crisis. I simply cannot imagine a version of London without any theatres – can you?
Let us to it.

Usually what I do is: I go back and see what was a box-office success in the past in order to get some inspiration.
So, let's see – which ones of mine did you like? Go on! You must know some of them!

Help the audience throw a few names around, and then a chorus of: "Yeah, that's not a bad one. Oh, I loved that one. Well, that was early days so sorry about that." If something not by Will: "No, that wasn't me, that one was Kit Marlowe."
Someone is eventually bound to say Romeo & Juliet.

Ah! Romeo and Juliet!

Lady / Sir [whoever said it], could you please be my Juliet? It'll help me tremendously to get in character. Don't worry, you don't have to do much at all. Just sit there. Yes! Exactly like that! Now, look at the sky. And – look like you're in love. No… love.
Fantastic! Phenomenal, thank you.

but soft / what light through yonder window breaks /
it is the east / and Juliet is the sun /
arise fair sun and kill the envious moon
who is already sick and pale with grief /
that thou her maid art far more fair than she /
it is my lady / o it is my love /
o that she knew she were /
she speaks /

she speaks /

You have to speak. Say something – anything will do.

she speaks / yet she says [whatever they said] / what of that /
her eye discourses / I will answer it /
I am too bold 'tis not to me she speaks /
two of the fairest stars in all the heaven /
having some business do entreat her eyes /
to twinkle in their spheres till they return /
what if her eyes were there / they in her head /
the brightness of her cheek would shame those stars /
as daylight doth a lamp / her eyes in heaven /
would through the airy region stream so bright /
that birds would sing / and think it were not night /
see how she leans her cheek upon her hand /

see how she leans her cheek upon her hand…?

Make them lean their cheek upon their hand.

o that I were a glove upon that hand /
for health and safety reasons
that I might touch that cheek /

Bravo! Well done to her/him, gentles! Thank you, my gentle friend, for being my Juliet.

Get a round of applause for Juliet.

It is very hard to play anything alone, and it is utterly impossible to play without an audience. I'm the one throwing words at you, but your imagination makes them all… compact.
And — that's what we need of course! Something about imagination itself! A scene in which we play on what is real and what is not and what is

theatre, and something metaphysical...

Think.

Would you happen to know of any good story having to do with a king, three daughters, love and imagination?
What, do you think I'm making up entirely new stories all the time? I'm writing three plays a year, no one can achieve originality on those deadlines! The adaptation is everything, of course. What would Romeo and Juliet be without Mercutio?
"A plague on both your houses! A plague on both your houses! A plague!"

Stab yourself with the quill and die a very dramatic and Shakespearean death.

That's some pure Shakespeare, right there!
It's a bit much, I know, but Mercutio is so melodramatic and flamboyant that his death needed to be just that. I also wrote that one after a bout of plague, so I thought that kind of thing would resonate with my audience – with you.
So now, how have you been coping with this outburst?
We are all used to the strange pestilence by now.
Still — it doesn't make it any easier, does it?
No.

I was born in a plague year, myself. I was the sixth child of my mother, and the first to survive past infancy. When the plague hit in 1564, she brought me straight to our family home in the forest of Arden and we sat it out there. I believe that's what saved me. My mum sang a lot, back then.

If you are able to, please sing this to the best of your ability. Should you have an easily transportable instrument, feel free to accompany the song with it.

It was a lover and his lass,
   With a hey, and a ho, and a hey nonino,
That o'er the green cornfield did pass,
   In springtime, the only pretty ring time,
When birds do sing, hey ding a ding, ding;
Sweet lovers love the spring.

If it went well: Thank you, gentles, thank you kindly.
If it did not: I'm sorry, but I'm trying my best. But I'm not the star of the show, you know.

I've always wanted to put more music in our shows, but my best mate Richard Burbage is constantly banning me from doing it. He says nobody will want to see a play composed primarily of musical numbers. Of course, he's saying that because he could not dance a proper jig to save his life! And I kind of have to do what he says – people come to see a Richard Burbage play, after all. He's the lead actor, the star of the show. Nobody comes to a play because it's been written by William Shakespeare! That would be ridiculous – can you imagine?

They still haven't properly accepted me in the big city. Particularly the University-educated pens – these ones assume that they're cleverer than everyone else because their parents are rich and they use a lot of big words. I can write big words too, you know!
Honorificabilitudinitatibus.
There! That's the longest word I've been able to come up with – and they're still not over it!

It was particularly tough on my rivals when I got my family a coat of arms. A beautiful, bright yellow one, with a black spear running through the middle. Oh, I know that my name is funny – so I had rather be the one making jokes about it. They've all tried to discredit me even harder since, simply because I am daring to climb their social ladder. You'll see, next up they'll try to start the rumour that I'm just a country ass who's incapable of putting two sentences together, and that surely such masterpieces as Hamlet or A Midsummer Night's Dream cannot possibly have been written by a goatish base-court gudgeon!

Well, my country life is proving a great source of inspiration, so buzz buzz to them! But — of course! Thank you! That makes sense — It's where we should look next!

This is done with the quill transforming itself into the fairy, and murmuring the words in your ear. The fairy is also propelling you throughout the garden.

over hill / over dale /
thorough bush / thorough briar /
over park / over pale /
thorough flood / thorough fire /
I do wander everywhere /
swifter than the moon's sphere /
and I serve the fairy queen /
to dew her orbs upon the green /
the cowslips tall / her pensioners be /
in their gold coats / spots you see /
those be rubies / fairy favours /
in those freckles / live their savours /
I must go seek some dewdrops here /
and hang a pearl in every cowslip's ear /
farewell thou lob of spirits / I'll be gone /
our queen and all our elves come here anon /

Magic is fantastic, isn't it? It makes life so much more wonderful when you believe in magic. And that was all thanks to my country education. I'm from Warwickshire—Stratford-upon-Avon, to be precise. Have you been?

Genuinely ask them if they've been.

Oh, you really should! It's only a two-days horse ride [adapt to where you are] North-West from here, and so peaceful – another world entirely. The river's clean, the streets are tidy, people are really friendly, some of our ale-houses are famous all over the country – I highly recommend the Dirty Duck.
I miss the Dirty Duck.
I mean — I miss my wife and my children.
I wished I could have gone to spend quarantine with them back in Stratford, but by the time I had put my affairs together, they had declared the emergency state: all but essential travel is banned, stay inside your homes, stock up on dried wheat and bum-paper... the usual.
Don't get me wrong, of course I was sad not to be able to go to them, but I'm not so foolish as to break quarantine. I'm not close enough to the King for that.... and what kind of excuse could I have invoked? An eye-test? I'm the greatest poet alive, and even I couldn't have pulled that one off.

I'm sending my wife some sonnets, of course. Her favourite will always be:

let me not to the marriage of true minds
admit impediments / love is not love
which alters when it alteration finds /
or bends with the remover to remove /
o no / it is an ever-fixed mark

that looks on tempest and is never shaken /
it is the star to every wand'ring bark /
whose worth's unknown / although his height be taken /
love's not time's fool / though rosy lips and cheeks
within his bending sickle's compass come /
love alters not with his brief hours and weeks /
but bears it out even to the edge of doom /
if this be error and upon me proved /
I never writ / nor no man ever loved /

Beautiful wedding sonnet, yeah, yeah.
Never told her I didn't write it for her.
Don't judge me! Marriage is complicated.
The more I think about it, the more I'm actually glad I'm not spending all this time in close quarters with my wife. I understand perfectly well why the divorce rate spikes right up after every plague.

Wan smile to people if they're obviously coupled up in quarantine.
"How's it going? Oh, but I'm sure you're doing just fine. It's obviously brought you closer together. So, so very close."

Maybe I should add more love sonnets to this new play? I got quite a lot of success when I published some of my poetry after the plague of 1593 — in fact, they're still being re-printed. And yes, if it's starting to sound increasingly like the plague marked my entire career and traumatised a whole generation — that's because it did.
You might think my sonnets sold out because humans are irrevocably fascinated by the great mystery of love, or because art is needed after a tragedy to help us translate our emotions into the cosmic scheme of things. But it's none of that.

Nah! They rolled off the shelves because the youths used them to get into their lovers' breeches and farthingales.

There's everything you need in there. Silly flattery: "The grass stoops not, she treads on it so light." Lines that will make them think you're a genius: "What I have done is yours; what I have to do is yours; being part in all I have, devoted yours." And then some for the pretty ones who wouldn't be able to remember a lot of by heart: "O! let my looks be then the eloquence and dumb presagers of my speaking breast." These do work wonders, let me tell you.

You know what you have to do to reignite that spark, gentles! Recite some sonnets to your lovers tonight! 100% Bard seduction guarantee.

So, where were we? Ah, yes — this play needs to please the youngsters, obviously. Well, they're the ones who fill our playhouses after all, and I'm a businessman if nothing else. So, what do you, young people, like?
(to the youngest member of the audience) Yes, you! I see you at the playhouse all the time! You really should be more careful with this young person's education.

Try to get a few answers out of them. Hopefully, someone will come up with something funny.

Comedy, of course! Yes, thank you! I need to break the ice with some comedy!

My teenage comedies were the best, the most to-the-point. There's one in particular which of course you know – a classic. I bet my best bed that it'll go down in time as a canonical masterpiece, same as my King John, and Troilus and Cressida and King Edward III! Absolute favourites.

Well... you know!

The Verona play!

Ah?

The one with the dog!?...
If no one says it: Yes — thank you to the gentleman at the back!
The Two Gentlemen of Verona, of course!
The hilarious scene with Launce talking about his dog Crab!
I need to fill the theatres, and what could be more quintessentially English than banging on about your dog?

look you / it goes hard / one that I brought up of a puppy / one that I saved from drowning / when three or four of his blind brothers and sisters went to it / I have taught him / even as one would say precisely / 'thus I would teach a dog' / I was sent to deliver him / as a present to Mistress Silvia / from my master / and I came no sooner into the dining-chamber / but he steps me to her trencher / and steals her capon's leg / O, 'tis a foul thing / when a cur cannot keep himself in all companies / I would have / as one should say / one that takes upon him to be a dog indeed / to be / as it were / a dog at all things / if I had not had more wit than he / to take a fault upon me that he did / I think verily he had been hanged for't / sure as I live, he had suffered for't / you shall judge / he thrusts me himself into the company of three or four gentlemanlike dogs / under the Duke's table / he had not been there / bless the mark! / a pissing while / but all the chamber smelt him / out with the dog // says one / what cur is that / says another / whip him out / says the third / hang him up / says the Duke / I, having been acquainted with the smell before / knew it was Crab / and goes me to the fellow that whips the dogs / friend / quoth I / you mean to whip the dog / ay marry do I / quoth he / you do him the more wrong / quoth I / 'twas I did the thing you wot of / he makes me no more ado / but whips me out of the chamber / how many masters would do this for his servant / nay / I'll be sworn I have sat in the stocks / for puddings he hath stolen / otherwise he had been executed / I have stood on the pillory for geese he hath killed / otherwise he had suffered for't / thou thinkest not of this now / nay, I remember the trick you served me / when I took my leave of Madam Silvia / did not I bid thee still mark me / and do as I do / when didst thou see me heave up my leg / and make water against a gentlewoman's farthingale / didst thou ever see me do such a trick /

Burst into uncontrollable laughter.

Ah, it's too good. Too good! The Queen laughed so much that we were appointed with a royal title there and then! Ah — such a masterpiece! Mark my words, this is why Verona will go down in history: the city where Proteus and Julia met, and where Crab the dog lived. My best bed on it!

I do apologise if that episode was slightly too unmannerly for young ears, my masters. But what can I say? like writing accessible, entertaining stuff. I don't want my plays to only be liked by scholars who have to study for years to understand what's going on — I want to write blockbusters that will fill the playhouses!

o what a rogue and peasant slave am I /
is it not monstrous that this player here /
but in a fiction / in a dream of passion /
could force his soul so to his own conceit /
that from her working / all his visage wanned /
tears in his eyes / distraction in's aspect /
a broken voice / and his whole function suiting
with forms / to his conceit / and all for nothing /
for Hecuba /
what's Hecuba to him / or he to Hecuba /
that he should weep for her / what would he do /
had he the motive and the cue for passion
that I have / he would drown the stage with tears /

and cleave the general ear with horrid speech /

make mad the guilty / and appal the free /

confound the ignorant / and amaze indeed /

the very faculties of eyes and ears / yet I /

a dull and muddy-mettled rascal / peak

like John-a-dreams / unpregnant of my cause /

and can say nothing / no / not for a king /

upon whose property / and most dear life /

a damn'd defeat was made / am I a coward /

who calls me villain / breaks my pate across /

plucks off my beard / and blows it in my face /

o vengeance / fie upon't / foh /

about my brain / I have heard /

that guilty creatures sitting at a play /

have by the very cunning of the scene /

been struck so to the soul / that presently

they have proclaim'd their malefactions /

the play's the thing /

wherein I'll catch the conscience of the king /

I believe that, you know. I believe that theatre can change a person. That it can wrench a soul asunder, crack it open, or make it whole again. I believe in a common human emotional experience. What is making this quarantine so tough on many is the lack of contact, of human contact. That's why we made our playhouse round, and called it The Globe. We're not a very subtle bunch. We wanted to make it clear to people that that's where they belong. That anyone can come to the playhouse, and see themselves in the actors on our stage. And in seeing ourselves, we hopefully learn, in turn, to be more human towards our fellows.

Everyone's expecting big and deep things of me now since I wrote that one,

my Hamlet. You might have heard of it? Oh, everyone loves Hamlet. It's almost as if some people like it better because it is so complicated: is he mad? Isn't he? Is it a real ghost? Does his mother know that his uncle, the new king, has killed Hamlet's father, Hamlet, the old king? What the farthingale are Rosencrantz and Guildenstern doing here?
It's as if I've made it purposely obscure.

Wink.

No, I just wrote it when I was in a really gloomy mood.
My father had just passed away.
And of course, my boy.
My only son, Hamnet, died a few years before that.
I had twins, you see. Judith and Hamnet, named after the neighbours down the street. Little Hamnet died when he was eleven.
We all taste grief. During hard times, we taste grief harder. His sister was never quite the same after that. No one was ever quite the same after that. But we're in the business of storytelling. So, I used it. I used my anger and my grief and my absolute confusion at the fact that children are allowed to die. I used it all in there. At least it gave me somewhere to put it. What's the alternative?
I do think that our preoccupation with mortality is another one of the reasons we come to the theatre. We know we do not have time to experience it all in one life, and we are eager to hear how others have fared. We come to see lives that are larger than our own — which is why I write a lot about Kings and Queens.

for heaven's sake let us sit upon the ground /
and tell sad stories of the death of kings /
how some have been deposed / some slain in war /
some haunted by the ghosts they have deposed /

some poisoned by their wives / some sleeping killed /
all murdered / for within the hollow crown
that rounds the mortal temples of a king /
keeps death his court / and there the antic sits
scoffing his state / and grinning at his pomp /
allowing him a breath / a little scene /
to monarchize / be feared / and kill with looks /
infusing him with self and vain conceit /
as if this flesh / which walls about our life /
were brass impregnable / and humoured thus /
comes at the last, and with a little pin /
bores through his castle walls / and farewell king /
cover your heads / and mock not flesh and blood
with solemn reverence / throw away respect /
tradition / form / and ceremonious duty /
for you have but mistook me all this while /
I live with bread like you / feel want /
taste grief / need friends / subjected thus /
how can you say to me / I am a king /

Times like these force us to think a lot about our own mortality. We only have a short time here, after all, and mine is dwindling rapidly. I am 41 already — I've got one foot in the grave!
Well, thank you kindly once again for your help, gentle masters and mistresses!
I do think my new play should be about a King, indeed. Makes for a nice metaphor, tickles the King's ego — and he's the one with all the shillings. As you know, King James is obsessed with witchcraft and witches. They aren't normally my cup of ale, mainly because I'm a reasonable person who is terrified of witches. But I have to write some in order to please the King — for his Scottish play. I'm going to make them as mysterious and weird as

I can, obviously — witches be witches.

Enjoy playing with this one – different voices, body postures, etc.

when shall we three meet again /
in thunder / lightning / or in rain /

when the hurly-burly's done /
when the battle's lost / and won /

that will be ere the set of sun /

where the place /

upon the heath /

there to meet with Macbeth /

I come / Grey-Malkin /

Paddock calls

anon /

fair is foul / and foul is fair /
hover through the fog and filthy air /

And yes, I know that "hurly-burly" is not a real word, but I really like inventing words. Some might even say it's "my thing."
Just like Ben Jonson's "thing" is satirical comedy.
I wonder what Ben is doing right now?

While we've been here, sitting in this [describe their yard] yard, he must have written three new comedies already.
Come on, Will, don't think about what anybody else is doing – focus!

A moment.

Ben mulls his own wine. I bet he's mulling some wine, and watching his sourdough starter rise exactly as it should.
To be fair to Ben, he does throw the best parties in Southwark. The frothy pox-marked varlot!

I miss Southwark.
The orchards and gardens, the brothels, the taverns and the inns — I highly recommend the George. I even miss the sound coming from the bear-baiting pits. The bear-baiting folk are our neighbours — that's where they have the bear-fights. It can be bear versus bear, bear versus dogs, which exits pursued by the bear… or one time they got one of the leopards from the Tower — that was something!
But that's the kind of entertainment we playwrights need to compete with! Tough crowd, London, these days.
It's not very hygienic obviously, and the plague has hit the district quite hard. I might try and move North of the river soon, but have you seen those prices?

Think, William, think!

This time last year, we were touring Kent, you know. Lovely place, Kent. The garden of England! I don't know if you've been to Dover, but those white cliffs, whose high and bending heads look fearfully in the confined deep, are stunning! High and bending head… that's good!
Oh, this is so exhilarating — we're getting somewhere! Is this what

productivity feels like? I had almost forgotten!

And while we were there, Richard had to get in a tavern brawl or two, for a change…

But of course — a good play always calls for a good fight!

I met up with Sir Walter Raleigh at the greengrocer's, the other day. He's a great fencer, Walter, and a decent chap. Oh, he's very melancholy, let me tell you. The quarantine's hitting him very hard. The man has just circumnavigated the globe, and now he's told not to leave his house but for essentials.

Back when he had just inherited that mansion by royal decree for services to the nation, he did not have anything much to do, and he often came to entertain us with stories of the Indies, of far-off islands, of mysterious kingdoms, of vast promontories… and also instructing the younger actors in fencing.

He's (mime the fight's figures as you perform it)

more than prince of cats / o he's the courageous captain of compliments / he fights as you sing pricksong / keeps time / distance / and proportion / he rests his minim rests / one / two / and the third in your bosom / the very butcher of a silk button / a duellist / a duellist / a gentleman of the very first house of the first and second cause / ah the immortal passado / the punto reverso / the hay /

Phew! That felt good! At least we're still allowed to practice fencing once a day, for obvious reasons.

Alright, so: some fencing, a bit of dagger and rapier work, perhaps some torture? Let's add a spice of treason as well — that's toying with the censoring line, but one simply cannot go wrong with some sensationalist treason and an atrocious torture scene or two. Got to compete with those

bears!
We're almost there! What else do we need?
What about the women? Let's put some women in this new play!
What? I know that some critics have said that I'm a misogynistic codpiece, but nothing could be further from the truth! Have you even heard Kit Marlowe's work?

I'm the one who wrote Queen Margaret:
when from thy shore the tempest beat us back /
I stood upon the hatches in the storm /
and when the dusky sky / began to rob
my earnest-gaping sight of thy land's view /
I took a costly jewel from my neck /
a heart it was bound in with diamonds /
and threw it towards thy land / the sea received it /
and so I wished thy body might my heart /

Portia:
the quality of mercy is not strain'd /
it droppeth as the gentle rain from heaven
upon the place beneath /

Viola:
o time / thou must untangle this / not I /
it is too hard a knot for me to untie /

Women actually enjoy a lot of liberties in London, you know. We're known the world over as "The Hell of Horses, the Purgatory of Servants, and the Paradise of Women." Tourists who come to see the sights leave absolutely flabbergasted at the way our women behave — they keep the houses and wash, brew, bake, scour, go to market, dress the meat and the drink, and keep their husband's purses. They also quite enjoy a pint or two in beer gardens in summer.

Oh, and you should hear the yells and cries of outrage at every performance of my Taming of the Shrew! When he plays Petruchio, Richard always ends up with nutshells all over his doublet and hose, and a rotten tomato or two down his back.

Women enjoy so many liberties these days — what's next? Being able to choose their own husbands?!

Laugh.

Sorry, ah — sorry. No. No. Took it way too far there.

I do believe you have given me enough substance to write a brilliant comedy indeed!
I thank you, ladies and gentlemen, thank you most kindly!

So, we've got: something about a King, treason, and a silly dog. The King should obviously be fighting to unite his Kingdom, as James is doing right now. The only logical thing to do these days to thrive as a nation after an international crisis is to form a union of some sort with your neighbours… Something about inspiration, and the wonderful trickery of the world, then a bit about tragic love — a marriage gone awry perhaps? We also have death and mortality, some magic, music and a bit of fighting. That is going to make for a wonderful play!

I'm thinking: The Most Lamentable Comedy of King Lear — why does this keep happening?! — King Leonardo His Three Daughters and Their Dog. And it should end on something hopeful for the future.
Because we all need hope these days.
A nice scene between the King and his favourite daughter. Something like:

come let's away /
we two alone will sing like birds i'the cage /
when thou dost ask me blessing / I'll kneel down
and ask of thee forgiveness / so we'll live /
and pray / and sing / and tell old tales / and laugh
at golden butterflies /

No —

gilded butterflies /
and hear / poor rogues /
talk of court news / and we'll talk with them too /
who loses / and who wins / who's in / who's out /
and take upon's the mystery of things /
as if we were God's spies / and we'll wear out
in a walled prison / packs and sects of great ones /
that ebb and flow by the moon /

Yes, yes that is very nicely put. Very nicely put indeed, if I may say so myself.

It's not very funny, though. Oh well, perhaps it shouldn't be a comedy after all? We all have a lot of healing and grieving and reckoning to do… maybe that is what the times are calling for.

Speaking of time, I hope you've enjoyed the one we have spent together as much as I have, gentle friends, and I humbly thank you for rekindling the fire of my Muse! It was a delight to devise such prolific sport in your garden, to drive away the heavy thought of care.
When this darkness passes, and I do not doubt that it will, I look forward to

seeing you all in our Globe playhouse again, on the South bank of the Thames!

I hope you have lovely summer plans ahead of you! Mine consist of finishing this play, trying to not drink ale too early in the morning, putting together the ultimate lute playlist to try to convince Burbage to add more songs to our repertoire, and finally managing to bake some decent sourdough bread. And so, I take my leave!

if it be true / that good wine needs no bush / 'tis true / that a good play needs no epilogue / yet to good wine they do use good bushes / and good plays prove the better by the help of good epilogues / what a case am I in then / that am neither a good epilogue / nor cannot insinuate with you in the behalf of a good play / I am not furnished like a beggar / therefore to beg will not become me / my way is to conjure you /

If you liked our time together, please tell your friends, relatives and anyone you know that the Bard is available to entertain them in their yards!

If you did not like it, please tell everyone I'm Ben Jonson.

Fare ye well.

Bow.

Finis.

THE SCOTTISH PLAY

A new play by Victoria Gartner

As William Shakespeare　　Adam Morgan
　　　　　　　　　　　　　　Arron Greechan
　　　　　　　　　　　　　　Alice Merivale
　　　　　　　　　　　　　　Brigid Lohrey
　　　　　　　　　　　　　　Caroline Mathison
　　　　　　　　　　　　　　Christopher Commander
　　　　　　　　　　　　　　Hannah Young
　　　　　　　　　　　　　　Jonathan Blakeley
　　　　　　　　　　　　　　Kaya Bucholc
　　　　　　　　　　　　　　Luke Farrugia
　　　　　　　　　　　　　　Rosanna Turner
　　　　　　　　　　　　　　Rupert Sadler
　　　　　　　　　　　　　　Will Harrison-Wallace

Directed by　　　　　　　Victoria Gartner

Produced by　　　　　　　Charlie Mackellar

Associate producer　　　　Beatrice Lawrence

Scotland Promoter　　　　Erin Rooney

Assistant Directors　　　 Aaron Blackledge
　　　　　　　　　　　　　　Runa Røstad Augdal

Godmother　　　　　　　　Dame Helen Mirren

World Premiere
May 2021

Produced by Bard in the Yard Ltd

THE SCOTTISH PLAY

Burst onstage / into the yard / garden.

Very happy to see people.

Come to the centre, take a deep breath, and:

Knock knock!

…

You all have to say "who's there?" Otherwise this won't work. This is a collaborative piece, I need you here, come on!

Knock knock!

Audience replies: "who's there?"

William Shakespeare!

Audience replies: "William Shakespeare who?"

… That's not really a joke, is it? No, that's just… well, that's just my name.

I can do better than this! Once more, with feeling!

Knock knock!

Audience replies: "who's there?"

The Black Plague!

Audience replies: "The Black Plague who?"

Pause.

… Too soon? I can tell it's too soon – that's alright.

Aaaargh! Doesn't work. Just doesn't work. I'm looking for a joke. A good joke.

This is an emergency! Absolutely – an actual artistic emergency!

Yes, I'm obviously trying to write a new play – aaaaaagain.

I'm here because I've heard that you like theatre in [address]. Is that true?

Some vigorous nodding …. Lovely, love that energy – I can feel we're going to get along splendidly, you and I. Well, since you like theatre, and you're here… and I'm here – we're all here!

Pause to reflect on this tremendous fact.

Isn't that exciting?

So, you will help me out with this, yes?

Yes?

Wait for them to actually say "yes."

By Jove's pancreas, that's fantastic!

You see, it's easier to figure out what you're feeling, or doing, when you can speak at other people for a while – it helps process your thoughts for some reason. (Proud) I actually invented that technique – a "soliloquy" they've been calling it. (Excited) I love it, it sounds very fancy! And you're welcome!

What's that? What have I got so far?

For this play, you mean?

Yes, of course, this play, the play that we will be writing together.

Well, I've got a speech – one speech – and it's still a pretty rough draft.

You want to hear it?

Ouh! I don't know… I don't normally do this – show my work in progress… Well, if you're going to help, I guess I should.

You keep this confidential now, right? I hear Ben Jonson has spies … *(Look around the place, murmur:)* everywhere.

What do you mean, you don't know Ben Jonson?

Now, that's incredibly suspicious! He's my main rival on the London scene! You know, Ben Jonson – big bloke, broken nose, carries daggers everywhere, has a cool tattoo he claims he did to himself? Very annoying? Ben! Eats seven roast chickens a day, goes for runs around the Tower, steals all of your mistresses, walks around with enormous scrolls of parchment he just keeps writing into with his pheasant-plucked fancy quill. Ben!

Well, he most certainly knows everyone.

I don't like this.

(Go to pack your bag) I don't like this at all!

What's that, now?

Ahhhh – I understand!

You've never been to a South Bank brothel, so you've never had the occasion to meet him personally!

Phew - fine! That's all fine, then.

Well, yes, sorry – I am quite twitchy about these things.

Now that I have a reasonably successful repertoire, if I may say so myself, well, some mongering threadbare jugglers are trying to get some credits for their own resumes! They're insinuating I didn't write my own plays! What a load of rubbish!

Have you read King John?

Seriously – who in their right mind would willingly claim to have had anything to do with that?

Well, I'm sorry! I'm only human, I cannot write smash hits all the time!

And when I'm stressed – I'm no good. I'm just no good! King John was one of those.

I'm a bit stressed, you see. This new King, the real King that is, if he is displeased with this new play, he said, he actually said that he might withdraw his patronage of our company.

We could lose everything!

And that's the best-case scenario.

If he's really, really not a happy bunny, all of our heads will end up on spikes on top of London Bridge! And yes, all of our heads! We're in this together now. You all agreed, remember?

Ah – I feel slightly more relaxed already knowing it's not all on my shoulders.

So, let's see – we will need a system.

I require… about 3… 3 volunteers.

You - great! What's your name now?

Name.

[name] - good name.

And… you! Name?

Name.

[name]. That'll do.   Aaand?

Name.

[name] - fantastic!

Thank you, gentle friends. A round of applause for our volunteers. Come on!

Applause.

Right, right, that's enough – they haven't actually done anything yet.

Let's see… You will need pen and paper.

What's that, [name]? No, I most certainly cannot give you my quill!

"Even so quickly may one catch the plague!", as we say. And as His Majesty has so solemnly proclaimed: we have to STAY ALERT – CONTROL THE PLAGUE – SAVE LIVES!

How come you don't have your own quill anyway?

No, I don't mind what kind, anything will do as long as you can write stuff down. Do you have anything you can take notes with?

If someone brings out their phone:

By Jove's furry bellybutton! What is this dark magic?

"Technology", you say it's called? Wow – what kind of a bird did you pluck that from?

Forget it, we don't have time right now – but you'll explain later, yes? I'm most curious!

So, my gentle friends and coerced volunteers, this is how it's going to work: you are all going to listen very attentively to whatever I'm blabbering on about in this…?

In this? …

Soliloquy! Soliloquy, [name]!

I've just said it! This is not starting very well. You're going to have to pay more attention than that if you want to keep your head, [name]!

So, you listen in – more attentively than [name], and you write down anything that you find inspiring. Or at least usable. Anything at all.

So, you write all of these things down, and at the end of this…

Soliloquy!

At the end of this soliloquy, I'll come back to you and we'll see what you've got – alright?

Phenomenal, thank you. We're all counting on you here.

Heads on spikes, remember? High stakes! Literally!

Now, time to focus.

The speech. The speech I've got so far goes like this:

Read from your notebook.

Is this, like, an actual dagger that I'm seeing right now,
The handle coming at my hand?
Come on then, let's be grabbing you.
Woah! I don't have you, but yet I can still see you.
Are you not a massively disastrous vision, a fearful
Thingy I can't quite feel or get? Or are you just
A dagger of the brain, a most fallacious erection,
Surging forth from the fiery… brain?
I see you still, yeah, in the very same shape
As my actual dagger, which I'm taking out right now.
You're giving me some directions, which is helpful,
And I was actually about to use a similar-looking dagger.
My eyes are made the chumps o'er my other senses,
Or I'm not called MacDonald
– weird name, I know, we'll work on it later –
Yep, I still see you,

And on your blade and on… the pointy bit,

I see some drops of blood,

Which weren't there before.

Nah, there's no such thing:

It's the bloody business which makes it look

Kind of like that to my eyes.

What, [name]?? I told you it wasn't finished!

I have to add way more "thees" and "thous." And I'll flip some words around, of course – so it all sounds better and, well, more 'me'.

What now, [name]? You still don't get a share of the profits, [name], no!

We went through this last year – I'm not the one in charge of the shareholders' contracts! Us writers, we're never really trusted with the money side of the operation. Even though I like to think I'm not too bad at it… money, that is. I've managed to put away a tidy sum during my career.

Actually, just recently, I bought the wife and kids a house.

(Very proud) I bought us New Place.

Fifty-seven quid that cost me! By Jove's hairy nipples! My wallet's still smarting from it. But what a house!

As a boy in Stratford-upon-Avon, as I made my way back home from school, I would see that big beautiful house, all brick and timber, every day. And every day I would think: "When I'll be all grown-up, I'll buy this!"

I've always dreamt big, me.

And I bloomin' well did end up buying it!

I was always supposed to train as a glover, like my dad. But that was never what I wanted. My biggest, wildest dream was a career... in the theatre!

When I was a kid, my encounters with the theatre were few and far between. But it made them all the more magical.

When the players arrived – ah! such a thrill. First, you'd hear their trumpets blasting, from miles away! And then – (Trumpeting sound) TUDUDUUU! - they would appear! Rolling along in a joyful procession, crossing the bridge over the river and into the town. They'd come straight to the Mayor's door to ask for permission to perform.

For a few years, that was our door. My dad, John, was the bailiff – that's how I got to go to school in the first place. He would allow the players to put on a performance at the Guildhall for the learned and greying heads, and then another one at the marketplace for the rest of us.

Now, those were my favourite.

Seeing all the town being brought together – to hear a play.

Getting to watch the scaffold being raised, and the player's splendid costumes, and most of all – listening to the words! Ah, the words! The words could make you see things you had never even dreamt of: far-off islands, ancient warriors, dragons, beautiful ladies! And they could make you, a little boy from the countryside, feel like you were a part of the story. Feel like you were a hero.

One time, I saw our neighbour Taylor, the baker, cry. Openly. He was weeping, right there on the marketplace, great big tears coming down his round strawberry face.

It was during a rousing speech from St George going to war. Later on, I used what I could remember from it. It went something like this:

no 'faith / my coz / wish not a man from England /[2]
God's peace / I would not lose so great an honour /
as one man more methinks would share from me /
for the best hope I have / o / do not wish one more /
rather proclaim it / Westmoreland / through my host /
that he which hath no stomach to this fight /
let him depart / his passport shall be made /
and crowns for convoy put into his purse /
we would not die in that man's company /
that fears his fellowship / to die with us /
this day is called the feast of Crispian /
he that outlives this day / and comes safe home /
will stand a tip-toe when this day is named /
and rouse him at the name of Crispian /
he that shall see this day / and live old age /
will yearly on the vigil feast his neighbours /
and say / to-morrow is Saint Crispian's /
then will he strip his sleeve / and show his scars /
and say / these wounds I had on Crispin's day /
old men forget / yet all shall be forgot /
but he'll remember / with advantages /
what feats he did that day / then shall our names /
familiar in his mouth as household words /
Harry the king / Bedford and Exeter /
Warwick and Talbot / Salisbury and Gloucester /
be in their flowing cups freshly remember'd /

---

[2] The Shakespeare excerpts have purposefully been left formatted as we used them in rehearsal. This method has been adopted by Victoria after a workshop with director Robert Icke. It consists of completely erasing the punctuation, which is a modern construct chosen by editors, and go back to the Folio of Shakespeare's works instead. Whenever there is a punctuation mark in the Folio, we signal it with a dash. This allows the actors to access Shakespeare's original rhythm more freely.

this story shall the good man teach his son /
and Crispin Crispian shall ne'er go by /
from this day to the ending of the world /
but we in it shall be remember'd /
we few / we happy few / we band of brothers /
for he to-day that sheds his blood with me /
shall be my brother / be he ne'er so vile /
this day shall gentle his condition /
and gentlemen in England / now a-bed /
shall think themselves accursed they were not here /
and hold their manhoods cheap / whiles any speaks /
that fought with us upon Saint Crispin's day /

Ah, listen to this! Of course, I wanted to be a playwright!

Oh, it didn't happen overnight – but I have never underestimated the power of dreams. Yes! By Jove's earlobes! You're helping already!

When you're stuck for inspiration, dreams are always a good place to start! I've also met some of my favourite characters in dreams, as it happens. Remember Mercutio, from Romeo and Juliet?

o / then / I see Queen Mab hath been with you /

peace / peace / Mercutio peace /
thou talk'st of nothing /

true / I talk of dreams /
which are the children of an idle brain /
begot of nothing / but vain fantasy /
which is as thin of substance as the air /
and more inconstant than the wind /

The wind, of course! Where else do you think stories come from, if not from dreams carried on the wind?

Wonderful – did you get that, [name]?

No more questions for now, please, [name], I'm in the flow!

This feels fantastic! For the first time in months, I'm officially in the flow!

I don't know about you, but I for one will happily admit it: it's not very inspiring to be stuck on your own for … (think, count on your hands, don't quite manage…) a long time! So this is really, really helping!

Because, yes, let me tell you kindly in your ear: contrary to popular belief, a plague quarantine is not the most conducive situation to creativity!

Oh, I've heard them all by now: Michelangelo painted the Sistine Chapel in quarantine, Caesar planned the conquest of Gaul, Ben Jonson learned ancient Greek and translated all of his works into the futtocking language… Give me a break!

Everybody thinks that all us writers have to do for the Muse to strike is to settle our buttocks upon a chair… stare out of the window a bit… sigh wistfully… exhale dramatically and… BAM! We'll be inundated with inspiration and smash hits! A ray of blazing light will pierce our forehead, and pour fertile literary brilliance directly from our brains onto the blank page – like a goose's egg flying straight out of her padded bottom – PLOP! We are writing! We are creating! We're an artist! A genius!

By Jove's gallbladder!

That is not how it works. That's not how it works at all!

Would you like to know how I write? Would you like to know how I, Master Will Shakespeare, poet, word-plopper, and all-round hit-machine, write? Do you want to know the big secret?

I flabbering work at it!!!

I write every single day. Have done for the last twenty-six years. When the Muse fails to show up for work, which is disturbingly often, well, when she doesn't come, I don't simply sit around all day staring out the window – shockingly, that is not how you manage to write two plays a year! No! I go out in search of her!

I go for walks. I go to my local pub – a lovely establishment called The Mermaid, I highly recommend it – and I sit in a dark corner and I eavesdrop on all the weird and wonderful conversations happening around me. Oh, I miss The Mermaid.

Then, I go to the market in Borough and buy myself a nice warm loaf and a pint of sack and I relish hearing the stall-sellers crying out about their wares and watching the fish-wives haggle over their stinky merchandise.

Then I might go to the sermons at St. Paul's Cross, and on my way back peruse what the booksellers are displaying that day – and I might even steal a line or two! That's not cheating, [name], that's called "borrowing." Us writers, we do it all the time. And when I should chance upon a copy of my own book, my Venus & Adonis, I very gallantly put it on top of the pile – ready for the next customer. Now that, we call that "building a reputation." Admittedly, the book doesn't really need it – it's been at the top of the charts for years now. I don't mind the royalties either.

"The plague is banished by thy breath…"

I'm sure you've read it, yes? You are people of taste, after all.

No? Oh, let me read you some of it, it's really very good – I'm awfully proud of it, had it published myself.

What? What do you mean, [name], we don't have time for this?

By Jove's turgid tonsils! How dare you accuse me of procrasti-writing?

Fine!

Fine.

Perhaps you're right.

(*Reluctantly*) I guess we should be focusing on the matter at hand.

But I can see you really want it. Yes, you over there, nodding, with the [describe what they're wearing] – so come see me after this, yes?

Wink.

Look, the truth is, I wanted to go through a bit of my poetry, because I'm not feeling quite confident these days. A writer… with writer's block. Not just any writer – London's most prolific living playwright –

Turn around.

Who said Ben Jonson?

Did somebody say Ben Jonson?

Hum. Right. Sorry, bit jumpy.

You see, rumour has it that Ben's just finished his Volpone – bollocking good title, that. It's set to be a blazing success, of course! He's already got a lead actor and an opening night all scheduled – By Jove's crusty toenails! Damn Ben flabbering Jonson!

Meanwhile, here I am – with my one miserable speech…

What if this is it? What if the Muse has decided to quit her job? Won't show up again?

What if I'm washed out?

[name] doesn't even want to hear my 1194-line poem anymore!

Flop down to the floor in despair.

Who am I if I can't write? I'm supposed to be the Master of Creativity!

The King of the Quill! The Top Dog. The Bees Knees.

The Bard!

Ah! This plague strikes, and look at me… A vagabond, a poor player, that struts and frets his hour upon the stage, and then is heard no more. This tale is told by an idiot, full of sound and fury, signifying nothing.

Sigh. Pause.

Sorry. Pardon me for being so dramatic! Force of habit.

And remember, please – if you do happen to hear me saying anything good, anything usable in a play at all, please write it down. Not always easy to sort the wheat from the chaff as a writer, you know.

What's that [name]? Not to despair. Focus on what we have. Yes.

Well, we have… we have a setting. That's easy – it has to be Scotland.

See… I haven't been completely honest with you all. As it is, I'm actually on my way back from Scotland. The King is expecting this new masterpiece the very minute I set foot on London's South Bank. So, obviously, I'm stalling. That's actually why I've stopped here on top of needing to ask for your help.

As you know, our new King, James I, is Scottish.

Apparently, he's descended from a line of Scottish Kings going back generations – originally from some guy named Banquo.

Anyway, since he wants me to write a play set in Scotland… I went to Scotland. To do some research. To get inspired. Well, my friends. Let me tell you what I've found out about Scotland.

It is cold.

Very cold.

Very, very cold.

And it is also… wet.

Terribly, terribly wet.

It is grey, and damp, and the food is very… sausage-y.

But the liquor – ah! Now, that's something else entirely. You've got to give Scots that, their liquor is not bad at all. Golden, and very potent. Not gonna lie – I've been drunk as a goat for most of my time up there. Which helped forget the food.

So, no, it wasn't all bad, really.

The Scots are very friendly, once you get to know them. I think they liked me because they like my plays. Especially up in Edinburgh. They like plays and players a lot there. Once the plague subsides, they were thinking of organising a big feast, with lots of plays, in the summer. A playeast? A feastiplay? I'll find a better word for it.

BARD IN THE YARD – THE SCOTTISH PLAY

There is something about Scotland though –

They are strangely proud of their witches! Don't get me started on the witches! Of course, I've met a witch, in Scotland. She was a surprisingly nice lady. Spawned from the murkiest pits of Hell, sure, but very well-mannered. We met her on the moor. Now that I think about it, the scene was set for it perfectly.

Richard and I were travelling at dusk on this dirt road. Yeah, Richard came with me – you know, Richard Burbage. Who is he? Duh, only the most famous actor of our times. Oh, come off it, you know who he is!

Anyway, we were pressing our horses, as we wanted to get to Inverness before nightfall, and we seemed to have lost our way.

She appeared – not appeared appeared, not out of thin air or anything! There must have been an explanation for it. In fact, I'm pretty sure she emerged out of the shrubbery. Anyway, we could have easily missed her if she hadn't spoken first.

How did I know she was a witch?

Well, she was singing a song as she was gathering her sage – witches love sage. It went something like:

(Sing this to Meredith Brooke's "Bitch")

I hate the moor today
The spell's so clear to me
I know but I can't charm
Tried to tell you
But you look at me like maybe
I'm an angel underneath
Innocent and sweet

BARD IN THE YARD – THE SCOTTISH PLAY

Yesterday I croaked

You must have been terrified

To see the darker side

I can understand how you'd be so confused

I don't envy you

I'm a little bit of everything

All rolled into one

I'm a witch

I'm a lover

I'm a child

I'm a mother

I'm a sinner

I'm a snake

And I do not feel ashamed

I'm your hell

I'm your dream

I'm nothing in between

You know you wouldn't want it any other way.

Bow.

We waited until she had finished – it was quite a catchy tune, and the polite thing to do – and then went through the usual:

"All hail, gentle lady!"

(In a Scottish accent, and imitating the witch) "All hail, William. Hail to thee, Richard Burbage!"

Richard didn't bat an eyelid at all this, since he's used to people knowing his name.

(Imitating Richard) "How far is it to Inverness, dear lady?" he asked.

I, on the other hand, was perplexed:

"You greet us with present grace, but say… from whence did you know our names?"

(Imitating the witch) "I know that the King sends you hither to write a new masterpiece, Master Shakespeare. Upon pain of boils. And your head on a stick."

"That is correct," I agreed, amazed.

She went on:
(Imitating the witch) "Well, you're the only strangers I have seen in these parts in a long, long time.

I put two and two together. And I predict that in future, you will be known throughout the land, William Shakespeare – The Bard!"

(Imitating Richard) "And me? How about me?" interrupted Richard.

She smiled gently with her hag-like face, and said: (Imitating the witch) "Lesser than Shakespeare, and greater. Not so happy, yet much happier."

Richard got quite flummoxed:
(Imitating Richard) "What the murky hell is that supposed to mean?"

(Imitating the witch) "Don't niggle me, Richard Burbage, or I shall curse this Scottish play forever!"

"Stop, man, that's not cool", I said, terrified at the idea of having a play of mine cursed.

But Richard, being Richard, went on: *(Imitating Richard)* "You imperfect speaker, tell me more!"

"The charm is firm and good", she smiled, and then, SWOOSH! She vanished into thin air! Or I think she did – there was a lot of mist.

Anyway, we went on and got to Inverness just as the sun was about to set.

She was obviously a fake witch. There's no way I'll be more famous than Richard Burbage, ever! But all in all, it was pretty cool. And invaluable research material.

We must put some witches in this play, of course! Well, feels pretty good to have that out of the way, actually. So now I've got 99 problems, but a witch ain't one.

There will be… let's see, three? Yes, three witches – Henry, Robert and Augustine. Well, they keep begging me to give them bigger parts, so that will do very well.

And no, [name], I don't know what we're going to do about their beards! Let's worry about that later, alright?

Let me finish this draft first.

We'll also add that catchy song – I do quite like songs.

Write down in your notebook:

"Witches and catchy songs."

Now, this is the stuff plays are made of!

Am I the only one writing this down?

[name]? What are you doing? Why aren't you writing? You better work, witch.

BARD IN THE YARD – THE SCOTTISH PLAY

Hmm. There are still missing links, though.

What's that, [name]? Are you saying we should have… a leading lady? On top of 3 witches??? Phew! That's… bold, but alright. Why not? To the deepest pits of hell with the critics!

A leading lady's easy – I've done lots before, we can come up with something good. Let's see… who was your favourite? Come on, you must know some of them?

Actually ask.

Yes! Juliet, Ophelia, Rosalind, Helena, Mistress Ford and Mistress Page, Queen Margaret, Viola, Portia, Olivia, Queen Anne – there are so many to choose from!

I will tell you one thing: I love writing the ladies. If we had more talented boys, there's no telling what I could do. Ladies are hostesses, mistresses, queens, nurses, wives, mothers, chaste maidens, hunters, adventurers, warriors.

And Cleopatra – Cleopatra is all of them.

She dies like only a Queen can die:

give me my robe / put on my crown / I have
immortal longings in me / now no more
the juice of Egypt's grape shall moist this lip /
yare / yare / good Iras / quick / methinks I hear
Antony call / I see him rouse himself
to praise my noble act / I hear him mock
the luck of Caesar / which the gods give men
to excuse their after wrath / husband / I come /
now to that name / my courage prove my title /

I am fire / and air / my other elements
I give to baser life / so / have you done /
come then / and take the last warmth of my lips /
farewell kind Charmian / Iras / long farewell /
have I the aspic in my lips / dost fall /
if thou / and nature can so gently part /
the stroke of death is as a lover's pinch /
which hurts / and is desired / dost thou lie still /
if thus thou vanishes / thou tell'st the world /
it is not worth leave-taking

Kill yourself with snake.

Die.

Wait until applause, give them the cue if need be.

Take a bow.

Thank you, thank you. I still don't understand why critics are so fierce about my lady parts. I find my lady parts absolutely delightful.

You see, I had plenty of inspiration – role models, so to speak. I was raised by a formidable woman. And my wife is pretty remarkable too. Not to mention that we were all governed by a Queen for years, and that was the most peaceful stint this blessed isle has ever seen.

I have always been fascinated by powerful women.

So how could I have anything but enchanting and powerful lady parts?

Three witches, and a leading lady it is.

Go to write it down on your own parchment.

Shake the quill.

What – this doesn't want to – umm!

Make a big splurge on the paper.

Oh – out, damned spot! Out, I say!

As you're trying to clean it up, it gets bigger.

Oh, oh, oh!

Oh no, now I have to wash my hands!

Wait – *(rummage in your bag)* – I think I have some – *(Take out cleaning wipes or some sanitiser and clean your hands.)*

There we go, no more of that. Alright.

Write down and say: "Lady part."

Fantastic.

And where there is a lady, there must be… There must be…?

Come on, team, this is an easy one!

Love!

Yes, of course, love. I'm good at that, too.

I've been in love a lot, you see. It helps.

And yes, I know what you're going to ask – have I been in love with a man? By Jove's grizzly moustache! Of course, I have!

I was very much in love with the Earl of Southampton. I also had a major crush on Kit Marlowe. What? I was never very subtle about it – or ashamed.

And I have also been in love with my wife. She was my first love, in fact. And she gave me children – wonderful children. Dear Susanna, and Judith, and Hamnet.

One love does not exclude the other. I don't really understand why it must. I just love… people, you see. I find everyone simply fascinating.

I've been in love at first sight – quite a lot.

What do you expect? I'm a poet.

Love is the easiest thing to feel, and the hardest to write about. But write about it, we must. It is one of those things we all share. It is the reason why we are here. Why any of us are here. We are all born thanks to this strange little God… blind Cupid, with his deadly arrows.

Beat. Smile.

Yes. I love love. Don't you?

And I love it even more when it goes wrong! Yes, by Jove's fetid liver! A clown in love – that's what we need!

One of my favourites is Dromio, in The Comedy of Errors. The plot of that one is pretty basic, as you well know – it was still early days, so: (please do this sentence in one breath) two sets of twins who each have the same name are separated at birth by a shipwreck and find themselves in the same city for one day, continuously being mistaken for each other by friends and neighbours and wives, because no one knows the master and the servant have master and servant twins with the same actual name.

One of the Dromios – the servant – is running back to one of the Antipholuses – the master – after a disturbing encounter in his master's twin's kitchens – still with me?

do you know me sir / am I Dromio / am I your man / am I myself / I am an ass / I am a woman's man / and besides myself /

marry sir / besides myself / I am due to a woman / one that claims me / one that haunts me / one that will have me /

marry sir / she lays such claim to me as you would lay to your horse / and she would have me as a beast / not that I being a beast she would have me / but that she being a very beastly creature lays claim to me /

she's the kitchen wench / & all grease / and I know not what use to put her to / but to make a lamp of her / and run from her by her own light / I warrant / her rags and the tallow in them / will burn a Poland winter / if she lives till doomsday / she'll burn a week longer than the whole world /

her complexion is swart like my shoe / but her face nothing like so clean kept /

her name is Nell sir / but her name is three quarters / that's an ell and three quarters / will not measure her from hip to hip / she is spherical / like a globe / I could find out countries in her /

Ireland sir in her buttocks / I found it out by the bogs /

Scotland / I found it by the barrenness / hard in the palm of the hand /

France in her forehead / armed and reverted / making war against her heir /

as for England / I looked for the chalky cliffs / but I could find no whiteness in them / but I guess / it stood in her chin by the salt rheum that ran between France / and it /

Spain faith I saw it not / but I felt it hot in her breath /

America / the Indies / o sir / upon her nose / all o'er embellished with rubies / carbuncles / sapphires / declining their rich aspect to the hot breath of Spain / who sent whole armadas of carracks to be ballast at her nose /

where stood Belgia / the Netherlands / oh sir / I did not look so low /

to conclude / this drudge or diviner laid claim to me / called me Dromio / swore I was assured to her / told me what privy marks I had about me / as the mark of my shoulder / the mole in my neck / the great wart on my left arm / that I amazed ran from her as a witch / and I think / if my breast had not been made of faith / and my heart of steel / she had transformed me to a curtal dog / & made me turn i'the wheel /

as from a bear a man would run for life /

so fly I from her that would be my wife /

The Bard laughs for a little while.

Ah, Dromio, Dromio and the kitchen wench! This is solid gold material!

Back when I wrote it, Will Kemp was our Dromio. Kemp! When he danced his infamous jigs in his very, very tight garters, no kitchen wench could resist him, indeed! Did you know that he was the one who made our jigs so popular?

We always dance a jig at the end of the play, now. It's a big, joyful reconciliation bit – just what you need after a tragedy. And not only to lift the spirits, but mainly so that the rabble that is our audience – no offence – doesn't go about stabbing the actor who played the villain later on in the pub, because they think he actually killed the pretty leading lady!

Yep, that's happened. It's not my fault people do tend to get very involved in my plays!

Anyway, we dance a jig. The jig marks the official end of our contract, of the suspension of your disbelief. Us players return to being mere humans again, and you, the audience, are brought back to the 'real world' – in which a player is not actually a clown, or a villain, or a Queen, or a witch, or even William Shakespeare.

Start clapping your hands to a rhythm.

We all unravel from the journey together, during the jig. It goes like this.

Clapping your hands, make the audience clap along to a rhythm.

Dance a little jig, still clapping your hands.

Take a bow.

Oh, that doesn't do Kemp justice, not by a long shot.

He passed away a few years ago, you see. And we are all the poorer for that.

There never was a clown quite like him, and there never will be again. The very fact of his showing up on a stage would make you laugh. His face – it was just his face. I remember him as Dromio – I remember it so clearly. He could make the very walls tremble with roaring laughter. Every time.

We went touring with The Comedy of Errors during that plague. Played inns and halls up and down the country.

That is always the first thing to happen. Whoever is able to escape London does, even though you're not perceived kindly by either side – by the ones who remain or the ones you might be bringing the plague to.

And if you want to leave, you have to leave really quickly. Once the number of deaths in a city district reaches forty, it is put in quarantine. Sounds familiar? It's from the Italian, quaranta -- forty. They kindly brought the word along with the pestilence, on one of their ships. Once a quarantine is in place, no one can escape. And it usually gets worse before it gets better.

You know the drill by now – you have to stay inside your home and open all your windows, since clean air helps.

What's that, [name]? Oh, don't be ridiculous! Don't believe any of those charlatan apothecaries who will try to sell you eyes of newts, or toes of frog, wools of bats or tongues of dog — no, those are completely useless. So is bleach – don't drink it!

Everyone knows that you must simply wear a mask, firmly pressed against your nose, and stuff it with as many oranges and cloves as you possibly can! The King's astrologer has assured us that this will very likely probably almost definitely prevent you from catching it, he hopes.

I understand it's been bleak everywhere. The worse is the uncertainty.

As you know, if one member of a household is found to have the disease, the entire house and all that inhabit it get shut inside by the constables, and a red cross is drawn on the door, signalling to all that they cannot enter.

You can hear the cries of those wretches, entombed alive in their own houses, waiting for the disease to take them, one by one… You can hear them from the streets.

And then one day, the cries stop.

That's when you see the old ragged ladies going in to search the bodies for signs of life, and on finding none, for signs of wealth. A poor tribute for that pitiful work. And amidst these scenes the physicians, cormorant men in their long Venetian masks, go about their gloomy trade to the sound of the knell, the ever-tolling knell, ringing for the stacking dead.

alas poor country /
almost afraid to know itself / it cannot
be called our mother / but our grave / where nothing
but who knows nothing / is once seen to smile /
where sighs / and groans / and shrieks that rent the air
are made / not marked / where violent sorrow seems
a modern ecstasy / the deadman's knell /
is there scarce asked for who / and good men's lives
expire before the flowers in their caps /
dying / or ere they sicken /

Pause.

Did anyone write that down?

[names of your assistants], anyone?

Thank you.

Listen to me! Here I am, in perfectly pleasant company, trying to write a comedy, and all I can think or talk about is these sinister times… by Jove's wrinkly elbows! It's so hard to snap out of it! Out of this… mood.

We have all been sad for so long now. We are grieving so many people, and so many things. Grief has torn us apart – it does that, grief – and now, we are afraid.

Afraid of the very air we breathe. Afraid of staying in one more day, the fences of our homes closing in on us like gilded cages. Afraid of going back out into the world, even after it has supposedly all ended. We are afraid of greeting our neighbours, of hugging our parents, of kissing our lovers. Afraid of what it might bring. We are afraid of each other.

That is the greatest tragedy of all.

Because I've missed you! I don't even know you, and I've missed you.

I've miss this – us! I've missed people.

No wonder I've been stuck for inspiration, going through a crisis of the plopping quill.

It's where most stories live, you see. Inside people.

Most of us don't realise this, of course. In fact, some people ignore the stories entirely, for most of their lives. Now, that's a foolish and rather dangerous thing to do, if you ask me. The stories we carry are our most prized possession. The treasure that allows us to connect with each other, with this world.

Plays make sense of the world because they tell the stories – our stories. That's why I write plays.

Writing tells the stories, and stories, in turn, create the world. It's a circle. It's spherical, like… a globe.

They have been around for longer than we have, you see. Stories were here first.

And they expect to be shown a great degree of respect as a result. If you treat them well – protect them, polish them, and tell them to those who can be trusted, to those who are willing to hear – stories will blossom in your heart like cherry trees in the warm spring sunshine. They will provide for you nectar, joy, softness, truth. They will give you eternal life.

Stories are a very powerful thing.

You cannot dabble in them lightly.

the lunatic / the lover / and the poet /
are of imagination all compact /
one sees more devils than vast hell can hold /
that is the mad man / the lover / all as frantic /
sees Helen's beauty everywhere /
the poet's eye in fine frenzy rolling /
doth glance / from heaven to earth / from earth to heaven /
and as imagination bodies forth
the forms of things / unknown / the poet's pen
turns them to shapes // and gives to airy nothing /
a local habitation // and a name /

The more you're ready and willing to grant them safe passage through you, the more they will keep on coming. For stories, most of all, want to be told.

Yes.

Gently smile.

I'm starting to remember… remember the way.

Thank you, gentle friends! Thank you so much. I do feel much better now. Ah – it is so much easier to start a fire when you have someone to help create the spark!

As you know, thanks to your help, I wrote King Leonardo – Lear! King Lear! - last year. Oh, it's a magnificent play – the dog, the three daughters, and I've also added prophecies, battles – and I added Edmund, of course.

My brother, Edmund, he died in the plague.

I keep on telling myself it was my fault.

He was young – so young. He had joined me in London. Edmund wanted to be an actor. You see, Edmund was different. He was born different. There was something wrong with his legs. He walked a little funny. And people in small villages in the country, especially kids, they did not like that Edmund was different, nor that he was funny. They were afraid of him. Called him names. Awful names.

So, as soon as he was old enough, Edmund convinced our parents to let him join me in the big city. He wanted, more than anything, to play. To play someone else – someone who wasn't him. Someone normal. Someone who would be accepted, who would be loved.

We made him play the women. We dressed him up in big robes and daring farthingales, and oh! She was fabulous, Queen!

He could sit, you see, and then, then all he had to do was speak. Because his legs had never worked properly, he had always made sure to work on his other skills. He had a voice like trumpeting angels, my brother. When he would speak, he would tear the air with sweetness.

And then the plague came, and took him first.

He kicked me out of the house – wouldn't let me in, not even to help him, not even to take care of him.

The last time I heard him was on the third night. I was sitting by our door, outside, in the mud. It was Spring. The air was warm, and the night birds had just started to sing. And then a voice joined them. A soft, very soft song came out of the window, in his sweet, sweet voice, [sing]:

our revels now are ended / these our actors /
/ as I foretold you / were all spirits / and
are melted into air / into thin air /
and like the baseless fabric of this vision

the cloud-capped tower / the gorgeous palaces /
the solemn temples / the great globe itself /
yea / all which it inherit / shall dissolve /
and like this insubstantial pageant faded
leave not a rack behind / we are such stuff
as dreams are made on / and our little life
is rounded with a sleep.

We buried him in Southwark Cathedral. I paid good money for a proper funeral, a player's funeral – enough to ensure that he would always remain there, on Bankside, in the only place on earth where he found some happiness, surrounded by the playhouses he loved so much.

And I added a part for him in the play.

thou nature art my goddess / to thy law
my services are bound / wherefore should I
stand in the plague of custom / and permit
the curiosity of nations / to deprive me /
for that I am some twelve / or fourteen moonshines
lag of a brother / why bastard / wherefore base /
when my dimensions are as well compact /
my mind as generous / and my shape as true
as honest madam's issue / why brand they us
with base / with baseness bastardy / base / base /
who in the lusty stealth of nature / take
more composition / and fierce quality /
than doth within a dull stale tired bed
go to the creating of a whole tribe of fops
got tween a sleep / and wake / well then /
legitimate Edgar / I must have your land /
our father's love / is to the bastard Edmund /

as to the legitimate / fine word / 'legitimate' /
well, my legitimate / if this letter speed /
and my invention thrive / Edmund the base
shall top the legitimate / I grow / I prosper /
now gods / stand up for bastards /

Yes. Plagues are times of change. Great change.

But we don't like change. Change is another thing we are afraid of.

Plague is a time of revolutions. In great turmoil lie the seeds of time. Who now can tell which grain will grow and which will not?

Are you writing this down? [name], [name], anyone?

Thank you, indeed. Don't miss the juicy bits, now –

Where were we?

Yes, revolutions need people. And theatre needs people… and people are not particularly welcome to gather in pandemics. Puritans are actually trying to turn this into an opportunity to close the playhouses, once and for all. Damn them, by Jove's bushy eyebrows!

It all began back when James Burbage – Richard's father – built a playhouse up North, in Shoreditch. Purpose-built playhouses, for the first time in our country's history!

Oh, plays existed before that, of course, but it was a hassle for the players, touring with all the scaffolds, instruments and costumes laden up on donkey-carts. It all seems very glamorous in the eyes of a young boy who's watching it, but when you're stuck in the middle of futtocking nowhere with a company of players who have not had a bath in weeks, and the donkey refuses to move from the middle of the road and decides to take a massive – anyway! Before that, plays were really processions, big medieval pageants, which you can still see in York if that's your cup of ale.

But there never was a proper space for it – not in England, anyway.

The bear-baiting folk gave us the idea, actually, since theirs were very popular. It's a central arena, and all around it, the audience can sit or stand and enjoy a refreshing pint and a moment of well-deserved relaxation after a long week of hardy work by watching bears, bulls, dogs or cocks fight each other to death in a flurry of fur, blood and guts flying everywhere. It all came from the Romans – these folks knew how to entertain!

It is very practical, the roundness. And it really helps with the acoustics!

You see, in here right now for instance, I guess it's alright because, well, it's just us.

(demonstrate these) But if I turn my back…

or look this way…

or that way … well, it becomes much more difficult for you to hear me.

Whereas at the Globe – ah, the Globe! – I can rely on the shape and the oak to just carry my voice through. And no matter where you are sitting or standing, you can see Richard Burbage's shapely legs in those tight garters! Genius, really!

And so, we built them! The playhouses! And we fought for them, tooth and nail! We built them outside of the Lord Mayor's jurisdiction of course – no respectable city-dwelling folk want celebrities for neighbours. We moved in to Shoreditch and the Southbank, side by side with our fellow lepers, prostitutes and boatswains. But the Puritans kept moaning and pointing fingers at us, mainly for stealing their audience. Why?

Well, it's simple, really: as we all know a play is performed at two in the afternoon, and so is mass – what's that [name]? Plays held in the evening? Nonsense, who would do such a thing? I mean, who could afford all those candles? We're in an economic crisis!

Anyway, which of those two would you rather attend?

That's what I thought.

But now, amidst the usual outcry about the squalid rabble that makes up our audience – no offence – and the boys dressed up as girls on our stages and how that is apparently inappropriate in the eyes of "up there!", they have decided that we might be also be the very source of the plague. The very source indeed! That our sins cried so loudly to the Gods that they have brought down this punishment for our crimes. A plague on their houses!

Well, if it's a crime to entertain your fellow humans, and make them laugh and cry and for one instant, one brief instant, to make them forget their own troubles and miseries – then it's a crime I am proud to commit.

That's what we are dealing in, here. Emotions.

And emotions are something we all need. It is the heritage we all share.

o all you host of heaven / o earth / what else /
and shall I couple hell / o fie / hold my heart /
and you my sinews / grow not instant old /
but bear me stiffly up / remember thee /
ay / thou poor ghost / while memory holds a seat
in this distracted globe / remember thee /
yea / from the table of my memory /
I'll wipe away all trivial fond records /
all saws of books / all forms / all pressures past /

that youth and observation copied there /
and thy commandment all alone shall live
within the book and volume of my brain /
unmix'd with baser matter / yes / yes / by heaven /
o villain / villain / smiling damned villain /
my tables / my tables / meet it is I set it down /
that one may smile / and smile and be a villain /
at least I'm sure it may be so in Denmark /
so uncle there you are / now to my word /
it is / adieu / adieu / remember me /
I have sworn it /

Remembrance. Rosemary – for remembrance.

I am talking about the dead a lot, today. I apologise.

Hamlet is always a tough one, for me. I wrote it in remembrance of my son.

Pause.

And we still seem to keep struggling with the comic element of all this...

Alright, Will, focus!

You're the Bard! You're the Bard! The Baaaaard!!!!

You've been stuck worse than this! You can do it – remember your dream, remember dreaming of being a playwright? Well, now you are one! And people are expecting a play, so pull your futtocking farthingales together!

Listen!

Listen.

Close your eyes. Pause.

What, [name]?

What am I listening to?

Not to my brain! No! Certainly not. That is the last thing you should be listening to, if you want anything remotely interesting to get plopped down onto the page.

Oh – and absolutely don't listen to that voice, that critical nagging voice – we all have that voice, mine's named Billy. I always say: "Thank you for your input, Billy." And then I keep writing whatever it was I wanted to write in the first place, anyway.

You have to listen for the fun things. For the adventure what will make your heart flutter in anticipation!

Shhhhh. Listen!

Close your eyes. Pause.

Oh, I'm so silly! We're in this together – so of course, you have to do it too!

Otherwise it won't work! Alright everybody, close your eyes.

Close your eyes!

Do you want this to work?

Close your eyes.

And only open them when I say so!

Make everyone close their eyes.

Close your eyes.

Hmmm… breathe.

BARD IN THE YARD – THE SCOTTISH PLAY

Yes… yes.

Alright… Listening in… Is this… Is this a warrior, a Scottish warrior? He's in a corridor – yes. It is dark – night. A new moon is in the sky, and stars are clouded o'er. I can hear the owl shriek. There are other sounds – clinking glasses, laughter. A banquet is happening somewhere in a room. Is this…

is this a dagger / which I see before me /
the handle toward my hand / come / let me clutch thee /
I have thee not / and yet I see thee still /
art thou not fatal vision / sensible
to feeling / as to sight / or art thou but
a dagger of the mind / a false creation /
proceeding from the heat-oppressed brain /
I see thee yet / in form as palpable /
as this which now I draw /
thou marshall'st me the way that I was going /
and such an instrument I was to use /
mine eyes are made the fools o' the other senses /
or else worth all the rest / I see thee still /
and on thy blade / and dudgeon / gouts of blood /
which was not so before / there's no such thing /
it is the bloody business / which informs
thus to mine eyes / now o'er the one halfworld
nature seems dead / and wicked dreams abuse
the curtain'd sleep / witchcraft celebrates
pale Hecate's offerings / and wither'd murder /
alarum'd by his sentinel / the wolf /
whose howl's his watch / thus with his stealthy pace /
with Tarquin's ravishing strides / towards his design

moves like a ghost / thou sure and firm-set earth /
hear not my steps / which way they walk / for fear
thy very stones prate of my whereabout /
and take the present horror from the time /
which now suits with it / whiles I threat / he lives /
words to the heat of deeds too cold breath gives /
I go / and it is done / the bell invites me /
hear it not / Duncan / for it is a knell /
that summons thee to heaven / or to hell /

(Open eyes! very excited and happy) YES! Ahahah! Yes.

You can open your eyes now – we've got it!

Write down with your quill, frenetic excitement.

"hear it not Duncan for it is a knell   that summons thee to heaven or to hell"

Who's Duncan?

Ah, I'll figure it out later!

This is… epicsome! Epicsome! Is that not a word? I don't care! Write it down anyway! That's how it's done, Bard-style! Hear me? Yes! Follow your heart! And don't be bogged down by such weighty and pompous considerations as grammar or words. Just make up new grammar, and new words. I do it all the time!

Write it down, [name], [name], [name], write it down now! Epicsome.

We've got something really fantastic – a very good beginning.

And we've got – what else have we got, then?

Ask your helpers. Repeat whatever they've got, as metaphors if need be. Make up story links.

Write some of the words down in your notebook.

Phantasmagorical! Ah – thank you! Thank you so much!

Now, let's see what we have got… this is a comedy about a big, moustached Scottish warrior who meets a witch on the moor and… seduces her by telling her the best knock-knock joke ever. And then a bit about a dagger. They will eventually have children, and their eldest will be sent to a bloody war in another country, be killed by his best friend and come back as a ghost. They will betray each other and… there will be blood… blood and more blood. And a sausage-y meal.

And [all the other metaphors you've written from your helpers].

Now, that's a good play!

Anything else?

Songs! We almost forgot the songs!

Great!

And it will be called….

It will be called…

THE SCOTTISH PLAY!

WOW! Fantastic title! Beat that, Ben Jonson!

Well, my dear friends, I must take my leave.

I'm sure you understand – I can finally go home! I can show my face on the South Bank, and complete this masterpiece. And keep my head from ending up on a stick! Our heads – all of our heads.

BARD IN THE YARD – THE SCOTTISH PLAY

You've saved the day!

I can never thank you enough for your help. I shall not soon forget it. Yes – you have shown me extraordinary kindness, even in these times of plague. Thank you again for letting me perform in your humble and odorous orchard, dear [name], [name], and [name]. And now, I bid you all …

Start clapping the jig rhythm again.
A small jig, echo of your previous jig.

… a very fond farewell.

Wink.
Bow.

Finis.

about
VICTORIA GARTNER

Victoria Gartner is an award-nominated writer, director and teacher. Over the last ten years, Victoria has written and directed work around Shakespeare's life and times in the UK, Switzerland, Germany and the Netherlands. She is the Artistic Director of Will & Co, which she founded in 2015. Victoria has been teaching Shakespeare for many years, giving workshops in festivals and universities as well as at the Shakespeare Birthplace Trust. She is passionate about giving everyone access to Shakespeare in a fresh and vibrant way. She has an MA in English literature with a specialization in Shakespearean studies as well as a degree in Dramaturgy and Directing. Victoria also writes poetry, non-fiction, and is currently working on a novel. She was born in Ukraine and she grew up in French-speaking Switzerland. In her spare time, she enjoys drinking wine, embroidery, and singing very badly.

victoriagartner.com